A Mother's Devotional

by Mimi Varberg

PRESENTED TO

____

____

____

FROM

____

____

____

Bite-sized meditations
from a frazzled mother
of pre-schoolers.

Dedicated

To my husband Tom
and to my daughters
Kara and Krista
The best friends I've ever had

This edition is published by special arrangement with and permission of Mimi Varberg, Bermidji, MN.

All scripture quotations are taken from the New American Standard Bible © The Lockman Foundation.

Earlier editions were published by Aglow Publications, first as *Tinker Toys & God's Grace,* © 1985, then as *Mischief, Messes and God's Grace* © 1986, and used by permission.

M36 Large Gift Edition ISBN 0-529-07128-2
M14 Slimline Gift Edition ISBN 0-529-06851-6

Book and cover design by Gayle Raymer

Published with World Bible Publishers
Printed in the United States of America

Contents

Introduction

Before I ever became a mom, I was overwhelmed by the awesome responsibility of parenthood. After Kara, our older daughter was born, I realized I hadn't even suspected the *half* of it. Then when Krista came along, the realization that I was in this game for keeps came thundering home to me. I was a mother of "two under two," and the strain was beginning to show around the edges.

I began to long for the day when my little ones would be old enough to converse with me, so I could begin teaching them and we could share ideas. Fortunately those times of longing are past because that fall, God shared a secret with me.

One day as we were sitting around the kitchen counter eating our grilled cheese sandwiches together, God showed me that he hadn't necessarily given me children to be their caretaker and teacher (although that is in part true). He had given me children to teach *me!*

That day was the beginning of a new attitude towards mothering. Slowly I began to see the equality of God's children in a different light. Even the youngest has something to offer the rest of us in areas of instruction, encouragement and love. I now see each of my children as mini-ministers sent by God to meet some need of *mine* in my spiritual journey.

I am also beginning to see God the Father through the eyes of my children. It is an exciting, often hilarious, thought-provoking experience! The meditations contained in this book were lived in the trenches, under fire.

They were written on the fly, and can be read on the fly. The first drafts had smears of peanut butter, finger paint and heaven only knows what else on them.

If you're a mother of young children, I stand here with you. I will not tell you that seeing my role of mother as a divine calling has made the day-to-day tedium of being home with young children a continual bed of roses. It hasn't.

But this I can tell you. If you are open to learning what God has to teach you through your own children, you will learn more, and grow more spiritually in these next few years than at any previous time in your life.

I am no longer anxious for my children to be any older than they are. I know each stage of their development will have something marvelous and unique to teach me. God will continue to use everyday situations with my children to teach, encourage, uplift and correct me.

Writing this little book has helped me understand the word *child* in a whole new way. I hope that reading it will do the same for you.

Spilled Milk—The Great Leveler

Whoever receives one such child
in my name receives me.
Matt. 18:5

To me there is nothing more exasperating than spilled milk. And being the mother of two children, ages two and three qualifies me to speak at length on the subject.

The first two times someone spills milk during the meal I handle it with the aplomb of a modern-day saint. But the third time, I come completely unglued, scrambling like a cat caught on the kitchen counter, and uttering the now famous Charlie Brown AAAUUUUUGHGHGHGH! How much, O Lord, is a mother to bear?

This noon after Krista's chocolate milk had gone over once onto the scatter rug on the right side of her high chair, and then onto the linoleum on the left side, I sat glumly chewing my grilled cheese sandwich.

As a fresh chocolate stain began working its way soggily into my right pant leg, I thought, *Let the little children come to me. Oh sure, Jesus, that's easy for you to say! Never once have I seen a picture of you holding a child on your lap when she has a glass of chocolate milk in her hands. The children in the picture with you are always clean, cooperative, and cherubic. Mine aren't.*

My spirit went from dingy gray to charcoal as I watched chocolate milk dribble out of Krista's mouth, down her chin, and onto her white T-shirt. Then I remembered.

I remembered the many times my angry temper has spilled all over the ones I love, running down the disappointed face of my husband or the frightened faces of my children. I remembered how each time my Lord knelt down, wiped the mess away, and with a smile said, "Oh child, I forgive you." And I was ashamed.

I stood up and began to mix Krista another glass of chocolate milk only to send it flying across the floor, its contents dribbling down the front of the counter and running into every one of the five drawers directly below.

I laughed! As I removed soaked dish towels, utensils, and napkins, I actually laughed!

Oh, thank you, Lord for spilled milk—for showing me how much like my children I really am!

Tell Me What You Think I Said

Now we see in a mirror dimly,
but then face to face;
now I know in part,
but then I shall know fully
just as I also have been fully known.
1 Cor. 13:12

At two-and-a-half, Kara was talking about God and Jesus. And I, trusting soul that I am, thought that when we talked about God and Jesus, Kara and I had the same Beings in mind. It was only during morning cartoons one Saturday that I came to see the truth.

Kara understood the idea of a trinity all right, but the three persons in it were Godzilla, Godsukey, and God-Jesus. My adult mind panicked and wanted to straighten the matter out for her, right now.

Then I paused. It was as if God said to me, "Wait a minute. She sees Godzilla as being kind and gentle. He helps people. He's strong and good. And he's a protector of the weak and powerless. That's enough for the moment. I'm in good company."

Oh mighty Father, Creator of the universe, how wise you are. You know just how much of your glory each soul can bear to see. Put a thirst in me to see more and more of your person each day of my life.

The Mouse

Truly I say to you,
to the extent that you did it
to one of these brothers of mine,
even the least of them,
you did it to me.
Matt. 25:40

Yesterday the neighbor children came over to spend the afternoon. After a while the oldest one, a boy, grew bored playing with the two younger girls.

"What can I do?" he asked.

"Would you like to color?" I suggested, reaching for the ever-popular, giant, 64-color box of crayons with a built-in sharpener.

"Sure," he said. "Where's the color book?"

"We don't have any," I answered. "Could you draw me a picture instead?"

"What should I make?"

"What do you like drawing best?"

"Mice!" he answered quickly.

"Okay, draw me a picture of a mouse, and whenever I look at it, I'll remember it's your favorite thing to draw. I'll think of you."

He beamed and began drawing a five-year-old's version of a girl mouse with a bow in her hair. "I can't help it if I draw girl mice best, he explained, drawing furiously.

After he'd finished the picture, I hung it on the refrigerator door and he left for home.

Today, he came back and headed straight to the refrigerator. He grinned when he saw that his picture still hung there.

Lord, help me to remember that all your children are special—that being a mother to young children also makes me a minister to their friends as well. Help me to encourage, uplift, and enrich all the little lives I touch just by being the "lady-next-door."

Perfect Healing

He will swallow up death for all time,
and the Lord God will wipe tears
away from all faces,
and he will remove the reproach
of his people from all the earth.
Isa. 25:8

The news came over the television while we were sitting at the dinner table. A deputy sheriff had been shot in cold blood by a young man who had grown up in my home town.

A wave of shock, grief, and anger swept over me. The deputy had been a family friend. My sleepy little hometown had suddenly become the scene of a grisly and violent crime.

Kara could see that I was upset. She wanted to know what was wrong. "A man just shot a friend of grandpa's, and he died," I said.

"Shall I pray for him?" she asked. I nodded and we all folded our hands.

"Dear Jesus," Kara prayed, "a naughty man shot grandpa's friend and he's dead. Please make him better..."

My mind raced. He's dead, he'll never be better. And then Kara finished her prayer, "And take him home to live with you. Amen."

At three years of age, she had prayed the perfect prayer. And I felt much better.

Lord, Jesus, help me to remember that perfect healing does not always involve a return to normal. That in the great sadness of death, there is always the promise of perfect healing as we come to live with you.

Dear Daddy

For you have not received a spirit of slavery
leading to fear again,
but you have received a spirit
of adoption as sons
by which we cry out, "Abba! Father!"
The Spirit himself bears witness
with our spirit that we are children of God.
Rom. 8:15,16

Four-year-old Kara folded her hands and bowed her head to say her bedtime prayers. "Dear Father," she began. "No," she said, shaking her head. "Dear Daddy, I ask you to bless over me while I sleep, give me good dreams, and wake me up with a happy face in the morning. Amen."

Dear Daddy! Abba! How naturally she said it. Father doesn't fit her vocabulary yet; it's still too stern and grown-up sounding. But, Daddy—now there's a word she can relate to.

A daddy is someone who's interested in her joys and sorrows. Someone who protects, teaches, and does his utmost to meet her every earthly need. Daddy is immediate, not far off somewhere. Daddy's girl...dear Daddy.

Lord, I confess that I don't call you Daddy very often. Help me to relearn about the special relationship that you and I have. Help me to learn that you are immediate, that your love for me does make me special. I want to come to you as a child, and with the confidence of a child say, "Dear Daddy."

The Nose and the Stomach

Bear one another's burdens,
and thus fulfill the law of Christ.
Gal. 6:2

There are many group activities I enjoy. Illness is not one of them! For the past few days both Kara and I have been ill. She has the stomach flu and I, a grade-A head cold.

Yesterday was the low point on the roller coaster ride into the pits for me. My face ached, my nose ran like a faucet, and my whole head felt like a rotten watermelon.

Kara, not sick enough to be kept down in bed, reached the pinnacle of owlishness and obnoxious behavior. She tormented her sister, cried at the drop of a hat, and insisted on lying right on top of me.

I thought to myself, *Why doesn't everybody just leave me alone! Let me be sick in solitude.* It seemed that the more I concentrated on my own miseries, the more miserable I felt.

And then the last straw. My husband went outside to shovel snow and to go to the store.

Deserted! That lucky dog, I thought. At least he's going to have a few minutes of peace and quiet. Despair.

Then I took a look at Kara and saw how truly pale she was. She was sick, too. She needed comfort. I had been wallowing so deeply in my own suffering that I'd disregarded her completely. So I made some herb tea, then we cuddled up on the couch and read stories.

The more concerned I became with her comfort, the better I felt. I found a blessing in bearing her burden; presenting myself a living sacrifice. Saint Paul was right!

Oh Lord, I am humbled. My sufferings are so small, yet I have a knack for making them seem so large. Jesus, help me to keep my eyes on the needs of others, beginning with the members of the family that you have so graciously given to me. I hold fast to your promise, Lord, that as we are a blessing to others, so we will be blessed in return.

Quiet Time

He leads me beside quiet waters.
He restores my soul.
Ps. 23:2,3

She had been sick with the flu for three days and was finally on the mend. After lunch I suggested we go upstairs and take a rest. I knew she needed some quiet time to help her recover completely.

Reluctantly she agreed, and we went upstairs together to have a little snuggle on my bed. We lay down, and after just a few moments she'd fallen asleep.

It's so easy for me to see when my children need rest and quiet time alone. Why is it so difficult to see my own need? Instead of taking advantage of the rare quiet moments in my day to just *be* quiet and let both body and mind relax, I too often race around like a whirling dervish, trying to cram as many projects as I can into a few childless minutes.

During that time I do glamorous things like scrubbing the bathroom, folding laundry, or the ever-popular cleaning the refrigerator.

When it comes to a choice between taking personal time and doing a chore uninterrupted, the personal time too often comes up as second choice. Do I, too, need someone to take me by the hand and lead me to a quiet place where I can rest? Yes, I do.

Oh Lord, I often miss your quiet voice because I'm too noisy and too busy to listen. Teach me how to rest quietly and then help me to take advantage of the available moments.

Be a Sharing Person, Mom

For where your treasure is,
there will your heart be also.
Matt. 6:21

One of the most often-quoted phrases in our house is "be a sharing person." My children are exhorted daily to share toys with a playmate or with each other. And I, in smug satisfaction, seeing that they do a more than adequate job of sharing, frequently pat myself on the back for the good job of parenting I am doing. One day, however, my ivory tower crashed to the ground.

For the past several months I had been writing down songs that I had previously composed. I had bought a notebook especially for that purpose, and I was proud of myself for finally gathering enough motivation to start the project. I even attached a special pen to my special notebook.

Kara came to me one morning and asked if she could draw. As I nodded yes, she disappeared into the kitchen to find some paper. Returning to the living room, she carried MY notebook and

MY special pen. I hastily took it from her, explaining that it was MY important book and NEVER under any circumstances was she to take paper from it.

She looked at me and said, "Be a sharing person, Mom." There was no anger, just a quiet phrase that left me exposed to myself for the miser that I was.

Conviction. Her things were as important to her as my things are to me, yet I had neglected to practice what I had preached—and a piece of paper, yet!

I ripped out a sheet, thanked her for helping me to remember, and put the notebook away.

Oh great Sharer, Oh, you, who even shared your only Son, help me to remember that people are always more important than things. Help me to remember that whatever we do for the least of these people, we do for you. Help me to share my time, my talents, and even my tablet with the least of them.

The Half-Given Gift

Do not lay up for yourselves
treasures upon earth,
where moth and rust destroy,
and where thieves break in and steal.
But lay up for yourselves
treasures in heaven.
Matt: 6:19,20

Grandma and Grandpa were here to spend the day, and after the evening meal in a flurry of hugs and kisses, they put on their coats and prepared to leave.

Suddenly I remembered a pair of fancy combs I'd put in Kara's barette box, and ran upstairs to get them for my mother who had long hair and wore a chignon.

As I handed them to Mom, Kara's face fell. "Mom!" she cried. "Those are mine!" My mother graciously returned them to her, and I could see Kara struggling with a decision as she sat on the stairs. The combs were too big for her and she'd never worn them, but they were pink—her favorite color.

Finally, she said, "Grandma, I'll save these and give them to you for Christmas." And I thought,

Oh, how thoughtful—how sweet. But before I could add another silent accolade, she grinned and said, "And then, Grandma, after Christmas is over, you can give them back to me. Okay?"

There have been times when I, too, have half-given a gift. I've done a kindness for someone with the thought that now she owes me one in return. I've placed my husband and children in God's hands only to worry about them when their welfare is completely out of my control. I've made charitable contributions but asked for a receipt as a tax exemption.

I wonder how God looks at these almost-given gifts. Does he look at me as I look at my child and think to himself, "She's got a long way to go before she's fully grown."

Lord, help me to give without ulterior motives—to freely give of the bounty you've given me.

Woman, What Faith You Have!

A joyful heart is good medicine,
but a broken spirit dries up the bones.
Prov. 17:22

Having worked at this career of motherhood for close to four years now, I have come to the conclusion that it must be a constant walk in faith. I am not only speaking about the Rock of Ages kind of faith that meets our needs when the big chips are down, but also about the nickel and dime, two-for-a-penny kind of faith of everyday life. Belief even in the face of overwhelming evidence to the contrary.

1. I have faith that a day will come when I will no longer stand dunking dirty diapers in the toilet.

2. I have faith that we will someday make it through a meal with no spills.

3. I have faith that I will someday eat my meals sitting all the way back on my chair.

4. I have faith that someday my house will not look like the toy department at Macy's just blew up all over it, and there will be no fingerprints

on the windows.

5. I have faith that even after the fifth straight day of rain and we've been cooped up for what seems like forever, and we're sick of each other and crabby, that the sun will shine again.

6. I have faith that the girls will learn that the kitty has legs and can walk all by itself.

7. I have faith that someday I will walk out the door on my way to a meeting without that gut feeling that there is food sticking to me someplace where everybody else can see it and I can't.

8. I have faith that the time will come when we all sit in church together as a family and I will actually hear the sermon.

9. I have faith that someday I will be absolutely alone in the bathroom.

10. I have faith that one day all the things that now drive me crazy about living with people will be remembered as the golden time, filled with love and laughter.

Lord, help me always to keep my sense of humor and to remember that it is easier to "soar" if I take myself lightly.

The Vinedresser

I am the true vine,
and my Father is the vinedresser.
Every branch in me that does not bear fruit,
he takes away;
and every branch that bears fruit,
he prunes it, that it may bear more fruit.
John 15:1,2

Krista has a strong interest in agriculture, and every plant in our house within reach and step-stool of a two-year-old is a living monument to her somewhat misguided ministrations.

She loosens the dirt around the roots, waters them until they are little islands in a sea of mud, and prunes them with the mercilessness capable only of someone under two. For some mysterious reason, the jade plant has been the most frequent recipient of her efforts.

There it stood, forlorn and almost leafless, a pitiful sight. Tempted to dump it in the trash,I decided instead to put it high out of her reach and give it one more chance. The once seemingly lifeless plant began slowly to revive, and at each place where a leaf had been plucked off, a whole new branch began to grow.

Many times I, too, have been pruned. Circumstances in my life have left me feeling almost friendless at times—stripped of self-esteem and confidence. In misery I have crawled off to be alone and lick my wounds.

It is at these times, however, that I have felt God closest to me. He picks me up, puts me in a high place and helps me heal. And I, like the jade plant springing slowly back to life, am made hardier and fuller by having undergone the pruning.

Oh, Master Gardener, you know what I can bear to lose, and you know what I need to experience, to gain fullness. Tend this branch of mine.

I Have a Bless for You

Pleasant words are a honeycomb,
sweet to the soul and healing to the bones.
Prov. 16:24

After prayers were said, a story read, and little Kara tucked in bed, I bent over, kissed her, and said a benediction. This ended her bedtime ritual.

Suddenly, she popped from under her covers like a jack-in-the-box and said, "I've got a bless for you, Mom." As I knelt there, she put her hand on my head and said, "God bless you and give you a healthy nose."

Although it sounded hilarious, I thanked her, turned out the light and went downstairs, touched by her child-like sweetness.

Being of Danish descent, I have inherited a very "healthy" nose to start with. I thought to myself, "If there is anything I don't need, it's a healthier nose."

It was only after going downstairs and having a few consecutive sneezes, that I realized what she had meant. She'd heard me sneeze, too, and had blessed my sneezing.

My definition of healthy had been entirely different from hers at the moment of blessing. She had seen my need more clearly than I had, and had responded out of love.

Lord Jesus, help me to see with clearer eyes. Help me to not let my blessings pass me by unrecognized because of a rigid way of looking at life. Continue to fill my life with the little blessings that make me the wealthy woman I am, and give me the vision to see each precious one. And, yes, Lord, bless me and give me a healthy nose.

The Dummy

Whoever slaps you on your right cheek,
turn to him the other also.
Matt 5:39

The other day Kara came schlepping into the house, almost tripping over her lower lip as she came. Her shoulders sagged. It didn't take the intellect of Ellery Queen to deduce that something was wrong.

"What's the matter?" I asked.

Eyes downcast, she mumbled, "Jeremy said I was a dummy."

For the first time in her young life, she had been the object of ridicule by one of her peers. The slump in those tiny shoulders showed the burden of feeling "not okay," of being in the "out" crowd.

I imagine the name had been called in jest, or at least not in the seriousness that it had been taken. But it had momentarily shattered her world. I knelt beside her, gave her a big hug, told her what a special girl she was, and that Daddy and I loved her, and that Jesus loved her.

"Let's color," I said and she brightened.

Soon we sat drawing together, the hurt forgotten.

Lord, sometimes I feel the same way. Sometimes the people around me make me feel not good enough, or that at least I'm on the fringe of their little group. I know you're my best friend and your love is the only thing I can really count on in this life. But it really hurts sometimes to be overlooked or downright ignored. My little girl-self comes to you with shoulders sagging.

Thank you for always giving me the comfort I need and for letting me know I'm special because you love me so much. And thank you too, that you help me to forgive the hurt, put on a smile, stand tall, and go out into life again.

I'm Not Going to Be Your Girl

"Cast away from you all your transgressions
which you have committed,
and make yourselves a new heart
and a new spirit!
For why will you die...
I have no pleasure in the death
of anyone who dies," declares the Lord God.
"Therefore repent and live."
Ezek. 18:31,32

Kara had been tormenting her little sister all morning, so I finally sent her to her room to think about her behavior. As I closed the door, I heard her holler, "I'm not going to be your girl anymore."

She threw herself on the bed and began to cry. Not a cry of hurt or of being sorry, but of sheer anger at having been punished.

I thought to myself, "Whether we like each other or not right now, doesn't mean a thing. And whether you want to be my girl or not is immaterial, too. You *are* my girl. I'm committed to you, and no matter how far away from my love you choose to go, I will always love you."

Suddenly, I felt as though God at that moment said, "And that goes for you, too!"

Many times I have chosen by either thought, word, or action not to be God's girl. A half-told truth, an angry word, deliberately ignoring a need around me.

At those times God puts me in my room to think about it; they aren't comfortable times, either. Not being God's girl is a miserable time.

A short time later, Kara's door opened. She came to me and said, "I want to be your girl again."

"You always were," I said as I held her close.

Dear Lord, I thank you that you are so committed to me that you died for my sins. And no matter how impossible I may act at times, you are faithful, loving me, and waiting for me to return—to be your girl again.

Teach Me How to Stroke Your Face

Let my meditation be pleasing to him;
as for me, I shall be glad in the Lord.
Psa. 104:34

They'd been in bed for half-an-hour. I sat alone in the living room listening to the quietness of the house. Gradually, I became aware of the sound of humming coming from above. As the sound grew louder, I realized that it was Kara. She was having trouble getting to sleep. I ascended the stairs, tiptoed into her room, and sat on the floor beside her bed.

We smiled at each other, and I stroked her forehead. After a short while, she began to doze off, then suddenly she opened her eyes, reached up and stroked *my* forehead. We sat, smiling at each other, stroking each other's faces, feeling our love for each other flowing through our fingertips. I was filled with a pleasure and a feeling of closeness that I'd never known before.

Dear Father, open my heart. Teach me ways that I can reach up and stroke your face when you're soothing me. How can I please you, Lord? How can I show you that I love you during those special times when I'm feeling that you're extra close? Those times make me feel so cherished and I want to show you that I cherish you in return. Teach me how to stroke your face, Lord.

The One-Ring Circus

"Truly I say to you, unless you are converted
and become like children,
you shall not enter the kingdom of heaven."
Matt. 18:3

The circus had come to town, and we bought tickets and went to take a look. To say the show was a small one would be an understatement.

How small was it, you ask? There was only one clown, and he also doubled as the trampoline act. The animals were old and tired, a perfect compliment to the rest of the performers.

My husband and I looked at each other and rolled our eyes. Barnum and Bailey, where have you gone? Little did we realize we were about to receive one of the bonuses God gives parents of small children.

Sitting with our little ones instantly transformed this sad, little circus into one of the most wonderful of sights. They watched with amazement as the monkey rode the bike. They whooped with laughter at the clown, and the trapeze artist in her bright pink leotard was the most beautiful lady in the world.

Then came the tiger—squeals! And then, the elephant—gasp! The biggest animal in the world picked up the most beautiful lady in the world (by the leg!) and swung her through the air! Cheers!

Then Kara, her nose wrinkled, turned to her dad and said, "He stinks!" More laughter. A circus that, when viewed through our adult eyes had been an object of disappointment and downright pity, was suddenly well worth the price of admission when viewed through our children's eyes.

Lord, thank you for the gift of second sight. Thank you for re-opening those doors of wonder and newness as I view life through the eyes of my children.

On Being a Grownup Person

But we all, with unveiled face
beholding as in a mirror the glory of the Lord,
are being transformed into the same image
from glory to glory,
just as from the Lord, the Spirit.
2 Cor. 3:18

Four-year-old Kara and I sat at the kitchen table doing a picture crossword puzzle—she, writing down the letters as I separated the word into separate sounds.

"Make the B this way," I said. "Not this way." I encouraged her when she was right, and corrected her mistakes.

After four or five words, she began to get silly. She guessed every possible letter except the one we needed to complete the next word.

I got up to leave, saying, "I'll come back when you're ready to be serious."

Her lower lip trembled, and her eyes brimmed with tears. "Mom," she said, "I'm not a grown-up person."

I wanted to cry. I'd been expecting six or

seven-year-old behavior from a four-year-old.

"You're right," I said. "Sometimes I forget you're only four because God gave you a good brain. Forgive me. Okay?"

Dear Lord, help me not to take the gifts you've given my children so for granted that I concentrate on the talent and ignore the child. Let my expectations for them be high enough to challenge them, but reasonable enough not to overwhelm them. I thank you that you are the model of the perfect parent. Thank you for challenging me while letting me know that you love me just as I am, even though I'm not spiritually a grown up person.

The Garden Angel

For he will give his angels charge
concerning you,
to guard you in all your ways.
Psa. 91:11

Freshly bathed, pajamed, and tucked into bed, two-and-a-half-year-old Krista said her prayers. As she finished, I asked the Lord to send her guardian angel to watch over her through the night.

Krista popped up, her blue eyes round, and said, "No, Mom, I have a *garden* angel."

"You do?" I chuckled, "Where is your garden angel?"

"In the garden," she exclaimed in a tone of voice that told me how silly she thought my question was. "He's gonna get wet," she went on.

"Why?" I asked again.

"Because it's raining out there." And with that, she snuggled down in her covers and closed her eyes, dismissing me for the evening.

She doesn't know what a guardian is, but she knows about gardens. She knows how we pulled weeds, cultivated, watered, and sprayed for insect invaders. As a family we watched over and cared for our garden all summer long, celebrating as the garden began producing.

Lord, thank you for my family's garden angels. For those divine beings who watch over us and protect us, unseen ministers guarding and guiding us as we grow.

Growing Pains

I, the Lord, am your healer.
Ex. 15:26

Kara had been waking up in the middle of the night with pains in her legs. She would wander into our bedroom crying, "Rub my leg, Mom, it hurts."

After several nights of this ritual, I decided to give her a calcium supplement. She eyed the tablet suspiciously. Up until now her only other encounter with pills had been her chewable vitamins.

She placed the tablet in her mouth, and with much gagging, gargling, coughing, and watering of eyes, she managed to get it down.

"Good girl," I said, as I handed her another.

Her eyes widened, and she backed away. "But Mom," she said, "it only hurts in one leg!"

I, too, suffer from growing pains. The Lord sheds the light of his Spirit on an area of my life and shows me where I need to surrender, or exposes a fault that has been hidden only from me, yet is obvious to everyone else. It is often painful and humiliating.

I run to him in those times saying, "Comfort me," and he always does. But sometimes his comfort is in the form of a "pill" that I have to swallow. Humbling myself, I must speak a word of repentance or apology before the Lord can heal me.

Too often my cry for comfort is conditional; as with Kara, it only hurts in one leg. I just want Jesus to make me feel better, but I don't want to be put through the pain of healing and growing.

Lord, lead me to a place where I'm not satisfied with just not hurting. Give me a hunger for your total healing in every area of my life. And thank you, Lord, that you will never be satisfied with doing anything less for me.

An Overdue Thank You Note

Do not neglect to
show hospitality to strangers,
for by this some have entertained angels
without knowing it.
Heb. 13:2

God did not make my mother a good housekeeper. I can walk into her house at any given time and write my name in the dust on top of the refrigerator or television. Books, papers, and general clutter abound.

No, God did not make a picture-perfect Ladies' Home Journal housekeeper of my mom. But he made her an A-#1 homemaker. Dozens of children have called my parents' home their second home. My brothers and I always felt free to drag a friend or a troop of friends home for dinner. There was always room and always a welcome.

Baseball gloves, ice-skates (depending on the season) littered our front entry. Mom called us a family of pile-its. We piled it there, and piled it here, any place there was room.

It is only after having become a mother myself

that I have seen the blessing of that house in disarray. My friends and my brothers' friends still visit my parents. It made me realize that, even when I was home, I wasn't the only person my friends came to see. My parents made each one feel welcome, comfortable, and completely free to be a member of our noisy family. Our childhood house was our home in every sense of the word.

Oh, Lord, thank you for my mother's house. Thank you that my children can go there and be their enthusiastic selves; that I don't have to worry about them spilling milk on Grandma's floor or putting fingerprints on Grandma's windows. Thank you that these things are taken in stride and remedied as they need to be. Thank you that Grandma's home is not the four walls and furnishings, but the people gathered there. And Lord, I never thought I'd say this, but thank you that my house looks just like hers.

The Most Beautiful Yellow

Submit therefore to God.
Resist the devil and he will flee from you.
Jas. 3:7

I stood in the kitchen washing dishes. Kara stood in the living room in front of her easel, a set of new tempura paints in the tray before her.

"Mom," she chirped. "I just dropped a drop of blue into the yellow and it disappeared."

Shortly, she said again, "I dropped some more blue into the yellow and it disappeared again."

A few minutes later she came howling into the kitchen, holding a bottle of pea-green paint.

"Fix it, Mom, okay?"

"Sorry honey," I said. "It's green now, and we can't make it yellow again."

"But Mom, that was the most beautiful yellow I ever had!"

I've had days like that. I've started out bright yellow, full of optimism and good will, and subtly, drop by drop, I've let the blues drop in.

Minor irritations, hurt feelings, a misunderstanding, an angry word, and suddenly I find myself in a pea-green mood and don't really know how I got there.

Lord, help me to recognize those drops of blue more easily and to cast them out in your name before they ever hit the surface of my bright yellow days. And I thank you, Lord, that you are the Divine Separator—that as far as the east is from the west, you can separate me and my sin, remove my blues, and make me bright yellow once again.

The Butterfly

But he was pierced through
for our transgressions,
he was crushed for our iniquities;
the chastening for our well-being fell upon him,
and by his scourging we are healed.
Isa. 53:5

I heard a simultaneous crash and scream come from the bathroom. As I rushed in, I saw Kara standing frightened half out of her wits. At her feet, lay our stained-glass window, bent and broken.

The window had been handmade, a butterfly—a gift from a dear friend, designed especially for us. Since we had received it, not a day had gone by that I hadn't stood for some brief moment of the day, watching how the light made the butterfly's wings glow, rejoicing in its beauty. Now it lay on the floor, dark and hideous.

Kara had climbed up to get a container of liquid soap I had placed on the same sill upon which the butterfly window had rested. She'd slipped, and pulled the window and curtain down with her.

Seeing she was unhurt, I chased her out of the bathroom, sank to my knees, and began to cry. I was sucked into a cyclone of emotions beyond anger.

Thoughts flew through my mind: I shouldn't have put the window there...we shouldn't have put the soap there...how will Roger feel when he learns that the window he made has been broken? Kids are always breaking and messing up everything!

As I looked up through the tears, there she stood, the most pitiful picture of dejection I've ever seen. "Do you still love me, Mom?" a tiny voice asked.

It was then that I really knew what it meant to hate the sin and still love the sinner. I thought of one Precious Spirit, fragile as glass, that had been broken by a thoughtless, careless world. And of a love so great it had allowed this Gift to be sacrificed.

With a constricted throat and brimming eyes, I said, "I will *always* love you. What you did has made me very sad, but I will always love you."

Lord Jesus, how much you love me! I caused you to die, and you lay broken for my sin and yet you still loved me. How unworthy I am, and how great my sin. Thank you for the gift of forgiveness.

The Grocery Cart

Train up a child
in the way he should go,
even when he is old
he will not depart from it.
Prov. 22:6

It was two days before Christmas, and I, two cherubs in tow, launched off on one last shopping trip before going to Grandma's house. Once inside the department store, Kara evaporated, and I spent the remainder of my shopping time looking for her. I was beginning to get the gnawing feeling that this trip was destined for failure

Next stop, the grocery store. Once again, inside the door my oldest began to wander away. "No, you don't!" I warned, scooping her up and depositing her in the front of the over-sized grocery cart.

Before my eyes, my sweet little pre-schooler turned into thirty pounds of screaming rebellion. Undaunted by the astonished looks of nearby shoppers, I snatched up a selection of fresh veggies and zoomed to the check-out stand, all this time trying to keep her at least half in the cart.

Because the store is one of those self-service varieties, I unloaded, bagged, and paid for my groceries with all this going on.

With my bewildered almost one-year-old hanging on, I zoomed through the door, Kara hanging out of the cart, screaming at the top of her lungs. When we arrived at the car, the situation only worsened. As I tried to put Kara into her car seat, she became as rigid as a two-by-four, refusing to assume any shape that could be made to fit the seat.

By this time I was wild. I'd taken all the nonsense I was capable of, so I turned her over my knee for several well-placed attention-getters. Unfortunately, I also succeeded in getting the attention of two carry-out boys. I looked up and there they were, staring into the car.

"Fine," I thought. "Now I'll be arrested for child beating, and this is the first time I've ever spanked her."

Finally I had her confined to her chair. She sobbed all the way home while I fumed.

Once in the garage, I walked back to her, knelt down, and said, "Should we ask Jesus to help us be friends again?" She nodded, and we prayed. Then she looked up at me and said, "I forgive you, Mommy."

I'm certain that I must have looked like a freshly-caught fish, my mouth going up and down, with nothing coming out. Then I realized,

I was just as in need of forgiveness as she was. I'd lost control, too. "Thank you," I said, "I forgive you, too. Hugs?"

Oh, Lord, help me always to realize the fine line between disciplining my children for their own good and giving them a whack just to make my frustration subside.

What You Need Here Is a Helper

Do not merely look out
for your own personal interest,
but also for the interests of others.
Phil. 2:4

I have aquired many ways of doing things from my mother. One second-generation household practice I employ is occasionally using an envelope or other semi-stiff piece of paper for a dustpan.

One day, after throwing her third consecutive dustpan of the season out with the trash, my mother loudly declared, "Any woman stupid enough to throw three dustpans out with the garbage doesn't deserve one. From thence sprang the envelope maneuver.

After lunch today I cleared up the fallout area under Krista's high chair, using my broom and a handy envelope. Kara sailed around the corner, stopped short, and after surveying the situation flatly announced, "What you need here is a helper."

Striding to the broom closet, she got out the

dustpan and held it on the floor for me to sweep into. I almost told her that I was practically done and thanks anyway, but seeing her eagerness to help made me keep still.

Working together, it only took me twice as long as it would have had I done the job alone. But seeing her march importantly to the garbage and solemnly dump the dirt in, then put the dustpan back and say, "There you are, Mom," made my heart thump with a mixture of pride and laughter.

And isn't that the way it is with God and us? He certainly doesn't need our help to do anything he wants done. He's God Almighty and could do it himself, thank you so very much. But he allows and encourages us to be his divine helpers, not only for the friend or neighbor that needs helping, but to let us have the experience of being needed, of making a difference.

Lord, help me to remember that whenever I see a need, it is not only an opportunity to help someone else, it is a chance for me to experience the encouragement and the feeling of making a difference that you've shared with me.

And Angels Hover'd Round

Truly I say to you,
unless you are converted
and become like children,
you shall not enter
the kingdom of heaven.
Matt. 18:3

They stood in two somewhat straight rows, faces shining, dressed in their holiday best—three-year-old angels in their first-ever Sunday school Christmas program. They came to tell the story of how the baby Jesus was born and about how much they loved him. In turn, each child recited his or her little poem, and the congregation applauded each one.

And I, mother of one of those little angels, got a taste of the joy of heaven. I felt myself transported to the side of the manger and to the foot of the throne at the same time.

Oh, Mighty God, who came to us as we are, weak and powerless, help me to keep Christmas in my heart in the way I witnessed tonight. As I stand at the side of your manger bed, let me always be three years old.

My Open It

If we confess our sins,
he is faithful and righteous
to forgive us our sins
and to cleanse us
from all unrighteousness.
1 John 1:9

She stood in the middle of the kitchen floor with a banana in her hands. "My open it," she said. My almost terrible-two-year-old was intent on peeling the banana herself.

I bent down to start it for her, and she pulled away belligerently and repeated, "My open it" with as much authority as a munchkin could have.

"Okay," I said, standing back to watch the debacle that I knew would ensue.

Tiny eyebrows knit in grim determination as she pulled at the top, twisted, pulled, and squeezed until mashed banana began to ooze out a side that had split open during the confrontation.

If she had let me give her a little start, she could have had perfect fruit, but she finally had to be satisfied with lapping mashed banana off her hands.

It gave me a feeling of mirth mixed with frustration. It also gave me insight. How many times in my life have I said, "My open it," refusing guidance from God, from family and friends in my struggle for identity and independence?

How many times have I had to settle for the "mashed banana" rather than the perfect fruit I could have had if I had let God make an opening for me rather than trying to squeeze one out for myself? And how many times have I eaten mashed banana and not even realized there was something better?

She finished her banana, ceremoniously handed me the skin, turned to me to have her hands and face wiped off with a washcloth, and said, "Thank you, Mommy." She turned on her heel, loping off into the living room to harass the cat.

Thank you, Father for always being there to wipe off the mashed banana after I have insisted, "My open it!"

Rest with Me

How often I wanted to gather
your children together,
the way a hen gathers her chicks
under her wings,
and you were unwilling.
Matt. 23:37

Most mothers have a built-in child alarm. I once slept through a storm where a tornado passed five miles from our apartment, but let one of my children make an unusual noise during the night, and my feet are running before they hit the floor.

Last night my three-year-old began coughing. It became almost continual so I went into her room to check on her.

"Rest with me, Mom," she said. I slipped into bed beside her. She took hold of my arm, and the cough slowly began to subside. As I lay there watching, she went back to sleep, but after each cough, I would feel pressure from her hand on my arm; even in sleep, she sought reassurance that I was still there.

As I lay there, I realized that I needed to be near her right then, too. I needed the closeness.

It was as if somehow my health would rub off on her if I stayed with her. I finally drifted back to sleep, but even in sleep, I was aware of the rapid heartbeat in the little body cuddled next to mine.

God is like that. He, too, wants to draw near to me when I'm in the "valley of the shadow," whether it is physical, mental, spiritual, financial—in trouble of any kind. He longs to let his divine presence rub off on me. My Father desires to hold me in his arms when I'm feeling small and frightened, to let me know how much he loves me, how concerned he is for my well-being. He yearns to show me how committed he is to my welfare. All I need do is ask, "Rest with me Lord Jesus, rest with me."

Thank you, Father, for drawing near to me and holding me close when I need it most.

Enjoy!

I urge you therefore, brethren,
by the mercies of God,
to present your bodies
a living and holy sacrifice,
acceptable to God,
which is your spiritual service of worship.
Rom. 12:1

They sat on the couch, their two little blond heads close together. Kara was "reading," to her sister, *The Monster at the End of This Book*, starring furry, lovable Grover from Sesame Street.

I stood, peeking around the corner, laughing to myself at the precious sight before me. I thought, *How I enjoy them!* When they play together and are happy, what an encouragement it is to my day. One of my favorite pastimes is just watching them.

How often I forget that I am also a child, created for my Father's enjoyment. I know how much joy I feel being his child, but does God enjoy me too? Does it bring a smile to his face when I'm living happily and I'm getting along with my brothers and sisters? Yes, it does.

Walking in his will for me will always place me in a situation of growth, and how much he must enjoy me when I do that, when I am happy in the confines of my situation.

Lord, help me to remember that I can be a source of pleasure for you, just as my little ones are a source of pleasure for me.

The Mouth in Search of a Meal

He will not allow your foot to slip;
he who keeps you will not slumber.
Psa. 121:3

My youngest daughter eats living things. Her sister, the kitten, and numerous houseplants have fallen prey to her over-enthusiastic teeth. Fortunately, none have perished, although there was one long distance call to the poison control center to assure myself that she wouldn't die.

There I stood, dialing with one hand and frantically extracting half-chewed leaves from her mouth with the other. My once robust jade plant stood leafless and forlorn, a silent reproach to my prowess as a tender of plants and small children.

After being reassured that the plant had done nothing more than supply her with a mid-morning salad, I heaved a sigh of relief. Then, just as quickly anger swept over me.

She hadn't stumbled over that plant. She'd deliberately climbed to get it. Urge to spank. Then a still, small voice, "She's only a baby. I gave her to you to care for. Be vigilant, and know that even though you may take your eyes off her, I never will." And I was thankful.

I thought of the many times in my life that I have gone out of my way to find the forbidden fruit, times when wrong has seemed more attractive than right, and how I, too, am always being watched by a loving God, ready to help me pick up the pieces when my world comes crashing down around me because of my disobedience.

Thank you, Father, that you never take your eyes off me.

Seizing the Moment

So teach us to number our days,
that we may present to you a heart of wisdom.
Psa. 90:12

I sat reading the paper as Kara and Krista tumbled around on the floor together. Suddenly Kara jumped up from the floor and climbed into my lap.

"Put your arms around me, Mama," she said, "cause I'm getting cold." I wrapped my arms around her and we sat there together swaying back and forth, enjoying the closeness.

"You know why I'm sitting on your lap right now!"

"No, why?"

"Because pretty soon I'm going to grow bigger and I'll be too big for your lap, so I'd better sit on it now."

I was stunned. She's almost four! She's right! It won't be very long until she *will* probably consider herself too big to sit on my lap. It seems like only yesterday that I could hold her in the crook of one arm.

Oh Lord, thank you for this shared insight. Time does have a way of slipping by unnoticed. Help me to seize the now and make it all that it possibly can be. I need to take the time to enjoy my children's early years—they're little such a short time. Don't let me miss one opportunity to cuddle, and snuggle, and giggle with them. Help me to seize the moment, so that when they're too big to sit on my lap, I won't have regret of opportunities lost.

He Did Anyway

Your Father knows what you need,
before you ask him.
Matt. 6:8

It had been a momentous summer. Kara had received a two-wheeler with training wheels for her fifth birthday, and we'd made many trips up and down the dirt road in front of our house. By summer's end, she'd gained enough confidence to want the training wheels taken off.

Restricted to the safety of our driveway, she dug in with a vengeance. Holding the bike to steady her at first, then letting go, I watched her wobble and fall, wobble and fall, up and down again. Occasionally she would walk away in tears of frustration.

Finally, the day came when she mounted and rode all by herself. I stood alone, watching my almost-kindergartner become self-propelled. I was proud of her, yet a little sad at the same time. It marked a passage for both of us.

All the next week she practiced getting on, riding and dismounting. On Friday afternoon she said to me, "You know why I could ride my bike without falling this week, Mom?"

"No, why?" I said.

"Because Jesus was holding me up," she answered.

"Kara, did you ask Jesus to hold you up on your bike?" I asked her.

"No, but he did anyway," she replied with a smile.

He's treated me that way, too. Many times I have launched out on a project without prayer for guidance or protection, to say nothing of inquiring whether it's his will for me to do it. Although I have not thought to ask him to undertake for me, he, in his abundant graciousness and mercy does it anyway.

Thank you, Lord, for your constancy. Even when we forget to pray and ask, you know our need and do it anyway.

Light in the Darkness

Even the darkness is not dark to you,
and the night is as bright as the day.
Darkness and light are alike to you.
Psa. 139:12

Krista, who had been toilet trained at one-and-a-half, suddenly at three-and-a-half began wetting and soiling her pants again. At first I thought there might be a physical problem, but she seemed in otherwise excellent health.

My concern developed into consternation, then anger, then finally to utter frustration. I chided. I scolded. I spanked. I made her wash her pants out herself. But I'd run into a brick wall. I felt completely in the dark with no light at the end of the tunnel.

Finally, I decided to do with her what I should have done right away. I took her to my room, lifted her upon my lap, and after we'd talked about it, we prayed together. Both in tears, we sought the Lord.

She prayed, "Dear Jesus, please tell me when I have to go potty. Amen."

I prayed, "Lord, I'm in the dark here, but I know that you know why this is happening to her. Please show me. Amen."

The next day about midmorning she came streaking around the corner, grinning from ear to ear. "Mama!" she shouted, "Jesus just told me I had to go potty and I *did*!" We both rejoiced!

A little later she crawled up on my lap and said, "Mama, I don't want to get bigger."

"Why?" I asked, mystified.

"Because I want to stay here and be your buddy."

A flash of insight. Her sister had recently started kindergarten and Krista's three-year-old mind was not ready to leave home. So in fear of growing up, she had begun to revert, thinking it would stop her from growing.

I told her she didn't have to worry about going away from home because she wasn't big enough. Some day when she was big enough, she'd want to go. Right now she could stay home and be my buddy for a long, long, time.

She was satisfied. God had answered the cries of both our hearts.

Father, I thank you for seeing it all. I rejoice, Lord, because even though I may be in the dark so much of the time, I know you never are. You are light, and in you there is no darkness at all.

Coming Home to You

Give, and it will be given to you;
good measure, pressed down,
shaken together, running over,
they will pour into your lap.
Luke 6:38

It was Kara's first day of kindergarten. As she climbed on the bus and it drove away, my eyes filled with tears.

I turned and walked back up the driveway and a still small voice whispered, "You've done real well at trusting her to me as long as you've been right there with her, but do you believe that I alone can keep her through this day?"

"Yes, Lord," I murmured. "Just help me when I weaken."

The day seemed light years long. At three-o'clock she exploded through the doorway, her entire body an exclamation point. She spoke in superlatives of the teacher, her room, the other children, everything right down to the bus driver.

After listening to an almost half-hour long litany of praise for the public schools, I asked her, "What was the best thing about today, Kara?

What was the very best thing that happened for you today?"

She thought for a moment, threw her arms around my neck and said, "Coming home to you, Mom."

With that one short phrase, five years' worth of frustrations, inconveniences, interruptions, and every other negative connected with being home everyday with pre-schoolers was marked: PAID IN FULL.

Lord, thank you, thank you, for this pearl. I'm going to put it in the treasure chest of my heart, and when the tedium of mothering and housewifery starts getting me down, as it does periodically, I'm just going to take it out and treasure it again and again.

And God Said

When he, the Spirit of truth, comes,
he will guide you into all the truth.
John 16:13

We were on our way down the stairs when my kindergartner turned and said, "You know, Mom, God didn't make the world."

Typically, I jumped to the nearest available conclusion, threw a mental poisoned dart at the public school system and thought to myself, *Ah! Just as I suspected—humanism has reared its ugly head in our household.*

I got ready to defend the faith. "Oh, he didn't?" I said trying to sound nonchalant.

"No," she replied. "He didn't have to make it! He just *said* it, and it *was*!" She turned and casually walked the rest of the way downstairs, leaving me open-mouthed.

The enormity of that statement hit me like a bomb. I recognized that this wasn't a five-year-old thought, and as far as I knew, she hadn't been discussing Genesis with any other adult. Although we had recently read the creation story together.

This incident has encouraged me to continue

sharing the scriptures even more diligently with my children. I am once again reminded that as young human beings some of the things children hear may very well go over their heads; but as ageless spiritual beings, their spirits can and will receive ministry through God's word. He has promised that his word will not return empty, but that it will accomplish that which he purposes.

Father God, I thank you for your word—a word that, when spoken had the power to call the very universe into existence, is yet so merciful that it can speak instruction and correction into my life without destroying me.

The Little Lord Mommy

From Christ the whole body,
being fitted and held together
by that which every joint supplies,
according to the proper working
of each individual part,
causes the growth of the body
for the building up of itself in love.
Eph. 4:16

At three-thirty I'd felt fine. At quarter to four I was stricken with a violent case of stomach flu. Shivering and nauseated, I sought refuge in bed.

At her bedtime, my youngest approached my bed and, after giving me a pat, offered, "Mama, would you like me to sing you a song?"

I nodded yes, and she began singing softly,

"Away in a manger,
No crib for a bed
The little lord *mommy*
Lay down her sweet head.
The stars in the sky
Looked down where she lay
The little lord *mommy*
Asleep on the hay.

The tears rolled sideways down into my ears as I lay smiling in the darkness. I felt the touch of a loving, comforting Father, who knowing just what I'd needed, tailor-made a love song just for me, and sent it forth from the mouth of my child. This truly was the Body of Christ ministering to itself.

Father, I thank you for the Body of believers that is my family. Oh, keep us in your ways, Lord, that we may continue to speak life, comfort and healing into each other's lives.

The Horse Who'd Be a Clown

Do nothing from selfishness
or empty conceit,
but with humility of mind
let each of you
regard one another
as more important than himself.
Phil. 2:3

It had been bitter cold for several days, and the girls hadn't been able to go outside to play. Bored and restless, they finally decided to put on a "circus." They spent most of their afternoon making preparations. They made tickets, found costumes and polished their acts.

The show was about to begin. Being the only other person home, I was directed to the choicest seat, and, before my eyes, a lesson in life unfolded.

Krista was the clown and Kara was the trick horse. The performance began with the clown amusing and amazing the audience with rolling eyes and uninhibited body movement.

After seeing what an enthusiastic reception the

clown had received, the "horse" must have decided that horsing around wasn't going to be all she'd expected it to be, so she, too, became a clown—trying to out do her sister in every way.

As I watched, my spiritual eyes saw through the outward action to a deeper truth hidden within. "All the world's a stage, and all the people merely players," Shakespeare wrote. Each of us in our own way tries to get our moment in the limelight even though it may be at someone else's expense.

I became convicted of the many times I, like my daughter, have been unwilling to wait for my turn to shine and have stepped on somebody else's stage, shoving them, however subtly, into the background.

Father, forgive me for my selfish insecurities and puffed-up pride. Teach me to wait on you, Lord, that I may become one who builds up my brother or sister rather than one who shows them up.

The Fortieth Anniversary

Let each one examine his own work,
and then he will have reason for boasting
in regard to himself alone,
and not in regard to another.
Gal. 6:4

It was a time of celebration, and my husband's family began arriving at his parents' nearby lake home. One of his sisters had arrived a few days early with her husband, three-year-old son, and eight-month-old daughter.

Being a very organized and orderly person, my sister-in-law became frustrated when her little girl decided to join in the fun and not sleep. After the third day of no naps and little sleep, my niece was doing fine, but my sister-in-law was exhausted.

On the morning of the party, she called, "Do you still have your crib up?" she asked.

"Yes," I answered.

"Could I bring Jessica over there after you've come out here so I can try to put her down for a nap in some peace and quiet? There's just too much going on around here."

My mouth said, "Fine, bring her over; the house is a mess though." At the same time my mind said, *Oh no! This woman vacuums for entertainment! Why couldn't it be the other sister-in-law, the one who is a casual housekeeper as I am?*

I could have written my name in the dust on the TV. I'd had two of the cousins for two days and the fallout from the four children's good time still remained. My entire house looked like it had been bombed.

As I hung up the phone, my first thought was to dash about madly and make an attempt to straighten up. But time was short and we were due at the cabin. So I heaved a sigh of discouragement and closed the door behind me.

My sister-in-law was getting ready to leave for our house as we arrived at the cabin. "The house is a wreck," I again cautioned her. "But make yourself at home and get some rest yourself."

"Well, if I get bored, I'll clean it for you." She laughed.

"Don't you dare," I said and cringed inside.

Six hours later I drove over with her husband to pick her and the baby up. The change was remarkable. She had left the cabin tense, irritable, and exhausted. She emerged from my house relaxed, rested, and smiling. The baby had slept the entire six hours.

On the way back to the cabin, she said, "You

know, for a while I thought it was Satan who had been keeping Jessica awake, but now I think it was the Lord."

"Why?" I asked incredulously.

"Because I had to come and be in your house," she said.

Seeing the baffled expression on my face she went on, "I've learned a lot about myself being here today. You and I are on opposite ends of fastidiousness."

"How kind of you to put it that way." I laughed.

"But everywhere in your house," she went on, "I found something encouraging to read. I felt like I could make myself at home. I found the bread and fixed myself something to eat, and just felt a real comfort there. Sometimes I'm so neat that I'm downright hard to live with. And I realized that there's more to a full life than having no lint on my sofa."

I experienced a mixture of emotions. First, I felt so good. It was encouraging to know that the spirit of comfort and welcome, which I believe is the Spirit of God, remains in our home even though we may leave it, and that his presence can be felt by others even though we're gone. And in that I rejoiced and thanked God.

Second, I was ashamed and humbled. I had not really wanted her to come because I had felt as though I were going to be judged on the outward appearance of my house. But God had allowed her to look with her heart and not with her eyes, and she was blessed. I asked God's forgiveness.

Thank you, Father, for placing us in the same family. We have something to teach each other thereby helping each other grow. Maybe she will learn to relax a little and I will learn to be more neat. But, regardless, we share an earthly family and you, our heavenly Father who loves and accepts us just the way we are.

The Dandelion

God sees not as man sees,
for man looks at the outward appearance,
but the Lord looks at his heart.
1 Sam. 16:7

She toddled across the room on sturdy, barely one-year-old legs. She and her daddy had been outside enjoying one of spring's first warm days. As she approached me, she held up her hand and there, clutched between grimy little fingers, was an almost stemless dandelion. Her face shone with love—and her eyes searched mine for approval.

I sank to my knees, held her, and wept. Others seeing that dandelion might have seen only a weed, but I had just received my first flower from my firstborn, and to me it was the most beautiful flower I'd ever seen.

Lord Jesus, sometimes my gifts of love to you seem so small. I'm afraid that others might laugh or make fun of my attempts to please you. But, wow! I know that in your eyes no gift of love is small—that you see through the gift into the heart of the giver. I thank you, Lord.

Please, Rock Me

Like a shepherd he will tend his flock,
in his arm he will gather lambs,
and carry them in his bosom;
he will gently lead the nursing ewes.
Isa. 40:11

She woke up crabby. At breakfast she decided, after the fact, that she had wanted her waffle cut in strips and not squares. She couldn't button her jeans and refused all help, and her little sister had just that morning discovered that she could drive Kara into a frenzy in a multitude of subtle ways. It had all the trappings of being a "white-knuckle" morning.

I was on the verge of setting her down and talking sternly about putting on a happy face or marching up to her room when she said, "Please rock me, Mom; I'm having a hard day."

I picked her up, and we rocked together in the big, squeaky rocking chair. No talking, just rocking. Silently binding up the raveled sleeve of care. It didn't take long before she was satisfied. Considerably cheered, she climbed down, ready to face the rest of the morning with a smile.

Help me to turn to you, Lord, when I'm having a hard day. Let me crawl up on the lap of your love and rock the crabbiness away. And Jesus, thank you for my family, for three sets of arms who always have a hug for me.

Come When I Call You

The Lord called Samuel;
and he said, "Here I am."
1 Sam. 3:4

My four-year old suddenly devised a new game for herself. Whenever I called her, she ran away and hid. At first it was funny, but as time went on, I became irritated.

I finally sat down with her and said, "I want you to come to me when I call you. I call you for a reason, and it's important that you come. When I call you, it doesn't mean that you come whenever you feel like it, or that you can choose whether to come or not, it means *come now!*"

Her blue eyes grew round and serious. She had gotten the message. And, as I said those words, they remained ringing loudly in my own ears.

Many times I have run and hidden when God has called me. Sometimes, I don't want to do what I know he's calling me for, so I have hidden myself in another "good work" to avoid his call. Often I have forgotten that the Father always has a perfect reason for calling me, that he will never call me for idle purposes. He calls me away from danger. He calls me to service. He calls me to intercession. And he sometimes calls me because he wants to spend some time—just he and I—alone together.

Lord Jesus, help me, like Samuel, to run to your beckoning voice.

The Widow's Mite

A poor widow came and put in two small
copper coins, which amount to a cent.
And calling his disciples to him,
he said to them,
"Truly I say to you,
this poor widow put in more
than all the contributors to the treasury;
for they all put in out of their surplus,
but she, out of her poverty,
put in all she owned, all she had to live on.
Mark 12:42-44

It was the Thursday before Mother's Day, and Kara couldn't wait any longer. Two days before, she'd offered me a stern admonition about definitely not looking in her underwear drawer because she'd hidden a surprise there for me that she'd made in kindergarten. The suspense, however, had proven too much for her. With a shy smile and her hands behind her back she approached me.

"I want you to have this, now, Mom." She pulled out a handmade card adorned with the traditional pink crepe paper flower. Inside were the words, "I LOVE YOU, MOM"...her name... and a carefully folded, well-worn dollar bill.

"It's my last dollar, Mom," she said, "But that's okay," she continued, "money isn't everything, you know."

She'd given all she had. I didn't know whether to laugh or cry, so I did a little of both.

Father, teach me again how to give with the generous abandon of a child. Loosen me up, Lord; I get so tied up with making ends meet that I sometimes forget to be lavish at those special times. Make me into a glorious giver, God, and keep reminding me that indeed, "Money isn't everything."

The Beauty of Cobwebs

Let the children alone,
and do not hinder them from coming to me;
for the kingdom of heaven
belongs to such as these.
Matt. 19:14

It was the day of Christmas Eve, and there was so much to do. I got out of bed with a yard-long list in my mind. After breakfast I started in with a vengeance, making up baskets of goodies to take to neighbors, preliminary dinner preparations, hit-and-miss house cleaning. And everywhere I went, Kara followed, a dog-eared book in her hands.

"Read it, Mommy!"

"Later," I said.

Christmas carols on the radio, peace on earth, dust flying, the vacuum cleaner roaring; upstairs; change the sheets for company; downstairs; clean the bathroom. And still she followed.

"Read it, Mommy."

"Later," I said, "Mommy's busy now."

Flour, sugar, butter, and eggs; Christmas bread

in the oven and the neighbor over for a coffee break. "Read a book, Mommy."

"In a minute." I said.

Along about lunch time pandemonium broke loose. Kara and her sister fought, cried, and clung to me.

Suddenly, I realized that during all the time I'd spent preparing "Christmas" for them, I had done nothing but ignore *them* for the entire morning.

We sat down and read a book. The dust on the TV remained.

Slow me down, Lord Jesus. Help me to remember that you came to us in a stable, not in a spit-shined house. You see our hearts, not the dust in the corners. Help me to make it Christmas every day for my little ones by giving them the most precious gift I can—myself!

The Most Perfect Gift

Whoever receives one such child
in my name receives me.
Matt. 18:5

This will be a very special Christmas for our family. Our shopping will be modest, but there will be many gifts present in our home that cannot be opened. Neither can they be touched, smelled, felt with our fingers or experienced in any other physical way.

The first gift is the gift of an open home. Christ has opened our doors this year and added a new member to our family. We now have a Vietnamese son and brother from a totally different culture than our own. His presence has already added a flavor—a richness—to our family that would have been impossible without him.

The second gift is the gift of open hearts. Christ has opened our hearts to love a son and brother that could never have been ours naturally. Although he has only been with us a short time, he is already dear to us. His laugh, the twinkle in his eyes, his sense of humor, already give us the same heart-warming feeling as the laughter of our own natural-born, little girls.

The third gift is the gift of promise. The Lord Jesus has said that whenever we receive one such child in his name, we receive him. I believe that. We have experienced a new aspect of Christ's presence in our home, through loving and caring for one of his children.

So, Lord, as you come into our hearts and home this Christmas, you are rather quiet, tawny-skinned, dark-haired and almond-eyed. And your name is Loc.